PR Superstar

- the ultimate toolkit for writing killer press releases.

2nd Edition, January 2013

By Susan Haswell © 2012

NOTICES & COPYRIGHT

This document is designed to be a simple guide to putting PR into practice. It is not intended as a training aid, nor will it replace the knowledge and expertise of a trained PR/Marketing expert. For all PR it is recommended that you consult with an experienced PR practitioner. Although every effort is made to ensure the accuracy of contents, the publisher/author accepts no responsibility for any errors or omissions. All rights reserved.

Some names and dates have been changed in the book due to timing and other sensitivities.

Health & Safety Announcement

PR can have far-reaching consequences, so with all your PR activities consider whether or not there are negative impacts from your story. If so, be very careful with any information you release to the media.

Front cover: Shutterstock/GoMangoCreative

CONTENTS

INTRODUCTION..7

WHAT IS PR? 9

THE TOOLS OF PR 20

GETTING STARTED - THE PLAN.....................................28

ASK THE AUDIENCE! 46

PUTTING IT INTO PRACTICE 54

CREATIVE IDEAS FOR YOUR PRESS RELEASE 57

WRITING THE NEWS STORY..83

THE PRESS RELEASE – GOLDEN RULES.....................89

A FEW EXAMPLE RELEASES...103

AFTER THE RELEASE..118

WHEN A JOURNALIST CALLS YOU 121

ADVERTORIALS 127

WEBSITES AND PR...130

EVALUATING PR 133

CHOOSING THE RIGHT PR AGENCY..........................139

PR JARGON BUSTER 144

ABOUT THE AUTHOR 151

Introduction

I'm making two big assumptions here:

One is that you are a busy person with little time to spend reading long books.

The other is that you probably want to get straight down to benefiting from the amazing results of public relations or PR.

So, save your luxury time to read the novel, thriller or autobiography that you are really going to enjoy; this brief guide to PR is designed to be quick, hard-hitting and get straight to the point.

Get the best from this book

This book contains a number of pen & paper exercises, and you'll get the best out of it if you actually *do* these… not just skim through them. Writing things down will help you connect with your gut reactions before your logical brain kicks in to rationalise your emotions. So grab a pen and paper, and spend a little time working through the questions; the results will be worthwhile.

What is PR?

Let's admit it, Public Relations, or PR, is one of those industries that everyone has heard of, but not everyone understands. Marketing and PR people have done a great job of keeping it shrouded in a veil of mystery. They want to make PR seem like a black art that shouldn't be tampered with at any cost!

This may upset a few agencies, but let's explode some PR myths:

- PR isn't the sole province of big brands, plc's, blue chip, or government-funded organisations.

- It doesn't cost a fortune.

- You can do it yourself.

- You don't have to quaff G&T, speak with a plum in your mouth or wear black all the time to use PR (though the G&T bit sounds fun!).

- PR isn't about "spin" or fabricating lies. It is a great way of promoting your business with very little cost, and has been used to launch and promote companies and products with great success.

So what is it then?

Succinctly, PR can be summed up as: "Establishing and managing a good business or brand reputation."

However great PR is also based on managing emotions. It's not just about getting cold hard facts across - it's also about how your organisation makes people *feel*.

So I would add: "*Great* PR is about building and maintaining *positive relationships*."

A lifetime to build and a second to destroy

A good reputation is not a thing you can buy or achieve overnight. First of all you cannot actually 'own' a reputation like you can own a brand name or logo.

A reputation is built on history, events, and those emotions that *other people* have about you. And when you realise that emotions could be a deep entrenched reaction, or a transient fleeting thought, you come to see that this reputation is actually only what's going on inside your customers' or clients' minds. Each and every one of them may have a slightly different idea of your business.

So yes, you could claim a "reputation for speedy deliveries", but if that's not everyone's experience of you then it's not actually your reputation at all - it's just a strapline. And if it's too much of a lie then imagine what that's doing to your reputation too?

So *every* organisation has a reputation, good or bad, whether or not it uses PR. To demonstrate this fully, please pick up your pen and try out the following exercise:

- Think about a company. Any company. It could be the restaurant you ate at last night, an internet retailer, your local garage, or any other organisation that comes to mind.

- Write down their name.

- Now think about your opinions of them:
  Do you like this company?
  What do they do well?
  Where do they fail?
  Are you looking forward to dealing with them again, or do you dread your next encounter?
  Would you recommend them?

Imagine if the company you are thinking about had the power to manage – or even *change* – your opinion of them. How about if that company was able to "intercept" your opinions? What if they could *reason* with you, before you made your mind up about them?

Consider: what if organisations could communicate openly and transparently with you? Imagine if they could somehow communicate that: *"the last poor encounter you had with them was because half their staff were working on a charity campaign to alleviate 3rd world suffering."*
Or
The receptionist was depressed because her boss had just been diagnosed with a terminal illness.

How about if the garage that deals with your car, was voted *"most honest mechanics in the country"* in a *Which* article?

- Would you feel more sympathetic?
- Would that change your *opinion* of them?
- Would they be *"managing their reputation"*?

Just as your feelings and opinions surface as soon as you think of a company, everyone who knows your company also has an opinion about it. Clients, suppliers, neighbours and staff. Whether your business reputation is good or bad depends on the opinions that these people (your audiences) form.

Public Relations can influence many things:

- Shareholders and share prices.
- Increase profits.
- Educate clients about your products/services.
- Improve staff morale.
- Increase the perceived value of your product/service.
- It can get you known.
- It can make you stand out from your competitors.
- It can affect a customer's decision to buy.

...Having a great reputation can even help you manage an emerging crisis!

The ultimate aim of public relations is about influencing opinions through providing 'news'.

Of course it helps that getting editorial media coverage is normally free of charge (compared to advertising) but there's another reason behind the power of PR - people are more likely to believe what they read in the media when it is presented as an article or news, than if it is an advertisement.

Welcome to the start of your symbiotic relationship with the media: you provide the media with well-crafted, interesting news articles for their titles, and in return they print or broadcast these stories which should help to promote your company.

What is News?

Another myth exploded: journalists won't run a story just because you've got a great relationship with them!

No matter how many people tell you that they "know so-and-so, who always runs their stories" it just isn't so. Most journalists have a high degree of integrity and intelligence, they know that to keep their readers they must provide them with real news and articles, not just "advertising fluff" written by their mates!

So, how do you get a journalist to cover your story? The simple answer is: provide them with news.

The most important thing about news is that it is *new!* It has to be something that people have never heard before and it has to be something of interest. Think of the things you've heard that make you say: "that's interesting, I never knew that, I'd like to know more."

Journalists always look for a reason to cover a story – and simply releasing information about a product isn't enough. Journalists have many sources to choose from before writing an article or feature for their publication or programme.

For your product or company to stand out, the story has to be something that catches the imagination, represents a new development for the company or the industry, has a strong 'human interest' element, or represents a fascinating case study.

Advertising v PR

When did you last buy a newspaper or magazine, or subscribe to a blog or ezine just to read the ads? With very few exceptions (like searching for a new car or job) most people do not refer to the media to read the advertisements.

PR messages have a higher credibility than advertising messages because editorial staff are perceived to be more impartial in their consideration of products and services than advertisers. In the minds of the readers, articles and news stories are simply more believable than advertising.

Although advertising, in some form, should be a part of any organisation's total communications strategy, PR can offer more credible, effective alternatives and even support advertising activity in terms of PR spin-offs.

Advertising is paid-for promotion whereas PR has no direct media cost.

What PR is not

Many people think that PR will take the place of advertising. It won't! There are many reasons for this, but here are the main ones:

- You can never guarantee that a press release will get printed. The only way to be certain your message is printed in a journal, or broadcast in the media is to PAY FOR IT!   And that makes it "advertising" or "advertorial" (see later).

- OK, so you get your press release printed, but will that ensure that your company logo is printed? Highly unlikely! Again the only way to ensure this is to PAY FOR IT!

- You want to get a specific message across. The only way to ensure that this message is delivered in full, and without being edited is to… Yes – pay for it! (That's why all product recall notices or public notices are advertisements, not only PR).

If it is important for you to get into a certain media, then the only way to absolutely guarantee it is to book the space and pay for it.

If your PR message is really hot news and you are certain it will get used, you still need to be aware that even the hottest news can be removed from the media if something hotter (or even a paid for ad comes along!).

Be aware that many trade publications or local publications exist entirely on advertising revenue. If you use these titles, then surely it is only right to expect to pay for coverage occasionally.

In short, don't dismiss advertising; think about using it to supplement your PR.

The Tools of PR

By now you could be forgiven for thinking that PR is just about media relations. It isn't. Media relations may be the most common form of PR, but true PR is about the entire communications mix.

There are at least 123 communications tools available to you, a list that is growing all the time (see the next chapter, Rule of Three). These tools include: sponsorship, one-to-one briefings, videos, emails, letters and, of course, media relations.

It is easy to fall into the trap of only using one or two activities, so make a real effort to try out new ones, and see how effective they are.

Use the "Activities and Tools" grid (later in this book) as an ongoing reminder of all these potential ways to communicate.

Bear in mind that even a single phone call is a communication tool and, as such, it can be used to influence someone's opinion!

The Rule of 3

Many different pieces of research over the years have shown that the most effective way to communicate a message is to ensure that you are using at least three different communications tools spread across the spectrum of media – print, personal presentation, electronic, video, audio, etc.

Try to recall the current TV advertisements for three banks and/or three lager brands. Can you even remember them all?

They spent a lot on those ads didn't they? Many tens of thousands in some cases. Yet, I'll bet you found it difficult to recall them.

So, when it comes to communications tools remember:

You cannot over-communicate – so use as many different tools as possible.

The following pages provide a list of potential PR activities. These activities are both communications tools in their own right, and they can be the inspiration for a press release. Either way they will give you some ideas on different routes to target your audiences.

To make the most of this list I suggest you transform it into a 3-column table for your own use. Column 1: Tool, Column 2: Audience(s) and Column 3: Success/comments. In the columns, mark down the success you are having with particular audiences, along with lessons learned.

Try to vary things; step outside your comfort zone and use activities you've not previously considered.

Activities & Tools		
Tool	Audiences	Success & Comments
Media Relations		
EXAMPLE: Press conference	*Shareholders*	*Successful for Q&As, great for feedback. Comments used in annual report*
Media Relations	Audiences	Comments
Press conferences Press releases Articles and features One-to-one briefings Interviews Background briefings/materials Photography Video News releases Online Press Office		.

Your own website		
Integration with Social Media		
Data capture		
Autoresponders		
Research		
Newsfeeds		
Ezines		
Testimonials		
Links to other sites		
Source of information		
Updated		
Relevant		
Research		
Organisations		
Public relations programmes		
Issues monitoring		
Results monitoring		
Focus groups/surveys		
Community Relations		
Direct involvement		
Events		
Sponsorship		
Donations to causes		
Meetings & Roadshows		
Posters/banners		
Visits and networking		
Website		
Community section/forum		
Direct contact		

Social Media		
Facebook Twitter Linked In Pinterest Quora Review constantly for new brands		
Internal Comms		
Videos/CDI/CDRom Briefings/meetings Newsletters Quality Guides Intranet/Extranet Case studies Feedback Direct contact Emails/letters Telephone Forums Training events		
Direct Mail		
Annual Reports Brochures/leaflets Customer reports External newsletters General literature Case studies Letters and emails		

Exhibitions (trade, virtual, public)		
Literature Sampling Demonstrations Audio Visual Stands & Displays QR Codes		
Lobbying		
One-to-one briefings Background Material Videos Literature Group briefings Ongoing contact Research		
Conferences		
Event management Audio visual Literature Entertainment		
Liaison		
Internal (counselling & coaching) External		
Internet		
Newsletters On-line research Email/website Community news and events Webinars		

Sponsorship		
Community events Individuals Sport Arts Internet Worthy Causes		
Financial Relations		
Annual reports Briefing materials One-to-one briefing Media relations Entertainment		
Corporate Identity		
Design Implementation Competition to design		
Crisis Management		
Training Planning Implementation		
IT		
Internet Intranet Extranet Blogging Training		
Training		
Volunteering Upskilling Seminars/events Webinars		

Special Events		
AGMs & SGMs Special occasions		
Advertising (PR Led)		
Corporate Product Launch Events		

It's a vast list - and it keeps growing as communications technology changes. The chances are that you are already doing some of these activities - but are you getting all the PR you could? Could you get better value by using different tools?

Most importantly - how INTEGRATED are all these tools and approaches? For example: at your next exhibition, do you have opportunities to collect feedback on your website? Have you got a team dedicated to responding to these comments? Have you printed QR codes on business cards that relate back to your latest offers?

Another element of PR is to be at the cutting edge of these changes; introducing new comms technology or being part of its evolution is an excellent way to promote your company.

Getting started - the plan

After reading through all these activities, your brain is probably full of ideas all clamouring for your immediate attention. It's tempting to crack on with them immediately. But before launching any PR or marketing campaign you will need to gather some very specific information to help you make some decisions.

- You need to decide on the business objectives of the campaign (i.e. make more sales, more profitable sales, new location, etc).
- You need to decide on how PR will help you do that (increase awareness of your product, launch new company, etc).
- You need to identify your target audience(s).
- Then you need to decide on your key messages.
- Finally - you need to decide the best* route to get your key messages in front of your target audience. *Best means taking into account your budget, the timescales, options available to you, audiences, etc.

Work through the following steps to help you launch an effective campaign.

Step one - your business objectives

First things first; PR can be great fun. It's wonderful to get lots of media attention and there's nothing to beat the adrenalin of a phone ringing constantly with media enquiries (OK, I've had a sheltered existence.) But putting the glamour and glitz to one side, it's vital to carry out PR for the right reasons – your business objectives.

There may be one or more business objectives; from raising awareness of a cause, to launching a new brand or preparing a company for sale. Consider the following possible objectives and expand your responses. The more information you provide the easier it will be to focus on making these objectives happen.

Try to estimate numbers, dates, people, etc, where appropriate. Use the 5 W's + (When, What, Why, Where, Who) and How (much/many) questions to guide you to a more objective and measureable response.
For example I might ask a client: *"Do you want to generate more sales of products (or time if you are a service industry?"*

And, of course, they would answer "Yes!"

But that's just not enough information to launch a campaign, nor to check whether or not it's effective. So I would dig deeper, with the 5W+ questions: See example below:

EXAMPLE RESPONSES

When? Before Autumn.

Why? To cover suppliers' increased costs.

What? Ranges A & B. Plus 20 hours per week more service time to be sold.

How (many/much/long)? At least an extra 40 shipments per month.

Where? Preferably within 50 mile radius of factory.

Who? More sales to retailers would be best, but extra online sales would help.

As you can see, by following this format of questioning, I've now got some firm targets and specific information to go for. I'm now narrowing promotions down to two ranges, to a timescale, and to target audiences (retailers, and online sales). Without drilling down like this, it's very easy to get sidetracked and miss the mark. The targets help too - I know what success looks like, and how close I am to helping my client hit it!

Take the following questions, use them with the 5W+ questions and really drill down to your own business requirements.

Potential questions to work through:

Do you want to generate more sales of products (or time if you are a service industry)?

Do you want to make more profit-per-product or per time unit?

Do you want to launch a new product or service?

Do you want to sell your business or acquire another?

Do you want to support a step in your business plan, e.g. appointment of a member of staff, opening up another office, etc?

Do you want to attract new staff members, new distributors, agents, etc?

Do you want to diversify or enter new areas of business?

Any other objectives?

Step two - identify your PR objectives

Just as you have now got a detailed picture of your very specific *business* objectives, you need to drill right down to specifics when it comes to identifying your *PR* objectives. Treat these as you have the previous questions and aim for as much detail as possible.

Example question, again something I would ask of a client:
- "Do you want to raise awareness of your brand?"

Of course they would say "yes" - after all, if nobody knows about your brand or product, then they cannot possibly purchase it…
However when it comes to PR, I want to know a lot more about the awareness my clients want to gain. So here's an example response to the further questioning:

EXAMPLE RESPONSES
When?   Before Summer.

Why?   To create greater brand awareness so it will be easier to launch another product.

What? All ranges, except the one we are going to delete soon.

How (many/much/long)? To at least the same online awareness as our main competitor attracts as a long term objective.

Where? Just the trade press and internet.

Who (to)? Trade buyers and through agents.

Here are some questions to work through, using the 5W+ approach for each:

Do you want to raise awareness of your brand?

Do you want to raise awareness of your product/service?

Do you want to raise the profile of your company, product or service?

Do you want to educate people about something?

Do you want to launch a product/service?

Do you want to gather opinions?

Do you want to support a business partner, distributor, etc?

Other PR Objectives?

Starburst mind-map

For both business and PR objectives you can use a "starburst" plan instead of a table. Enter your primary goal in the centre of a 6-point star, then add one of the following words to each point: **When?, why?, what?, how?, where?, who?**

Expand your star points, to transform it into a mind-map, eg: your central goal may read: "Win more business" in the middle of the star, then under the "who" point, you could include:

Who *to?* - existing customers, our database, our network targets.
Who *for?* - for all our staff so we can retain everyone.
Who *will do it?* - we can recruit a new person.

This starburst route is great for group brainstorms too as it offers flexibility for everyone to get involved and often raises more questions along the way.

Bear in mind that these objectives may well change, however keeping an initial plan of them and checking back will help you see where you've come from - and why.

Tip: Schedule a frequent check on objectives, at least once every 6 months.

Step three - identify your targets

Your targets or target audiences are the people you would like to communicate with.

"If your press release appears in a newspaper that your target audience doesn't read, does it make any noise?"

The answer is probably "not much". However journalists of one media will sometimes read other media for information - so if you run a piece in a local paper, you may get it picked up in a national. As you can imagine, this is a long winded way of going round things and your message is likely to be well diluted by a few rounds of editing. So cut to the chase: identify your targets and aim for them directly for the most efficient and effective impact.

Start by asking yourself these questions:

*What business sector am I in?

Who are my main clients?

What size/type of industry do we serve?

What size/types of industry would we like to serve?

What is the geographical location of the clients we serve?

What locations do we want to target?

Where would our target clients hear about us?

Now you have completed this exercise, go back to question one* and re-consider: ***are you really only in the sector you have identified?***

For example.   If you are a restaurant owner, you could have answered with "hospitality". But think again…

Couldn't you also be in:

- Leisure?
- Tourism?
- Food & drink?
- Events?
- Venues
- Entertainment?
- Business services?
- Music?
- IT (for an internet café)?
- Arts (if you display arts in your establishment)?
- Training (if you train your staff/take on apprentices)?

The more additional sectors you can apply to your business, the wider the PR story you will have, the more sectors of media, magazines and newsletters that you can make your business appeal to.

Another bonus of adding notional sectors to your business is that they will help you to think more creatively about your company. What other things you could be doing. Other markets you could tackle.

And once you have added to your sectors, you will find it useful to go through the rest of this questionnaire again, addressing the other elements to fit in with your new-found business breadth.

The Influencers

The previous exercise will have helped you consider where to find your target client base(s) but there are additional audiences that you need to take into account. These are your "influencers". They may never place an order with you, but the way that they think and talk about you may influence massive orders coming your way - or not…

- Staff: do you need to communicate with your staff more?

- Neighbours – what do they know about you?

- Recommenders - like your bank/advisors, etc.

- Suppliers, agents, distributors, wholesalers – they may be in touch with your customers too.

- Local MP, councillor, dignitaries or those in office.

- Trade bodies and associations.

Answer these questions honestly. Ask colleagues to answer them too; they may have a different slant on the whole picture.

It may seem vague, but it pays to look at future influencers too. For example, if there are new trends or causes coming to bear on a marketplace, consider where they have come from and who is influencing them. A good example can be the effect of pressure groups on pharmaceuticals companies. With new technologies developing, there also are more lobbyists, pressure groups and interested parties. Keeping an eye out to see who is involved with various groups, and ensuring you are communicating with them can help you expand your message.

Step four - refine your key messages

Before you start communicating, you need to decide what your key messages are. A *Key Message* is not a strapline, or an advertising slogan. It is a plain simple statement about your company.

For example*: "We are a local company employing highly trained people, to provide and install quality air conditioning equipment"*

Aim to find several key messages; different audiences will need to hear different things about your company. Ask yourself:

"What are our CPBs?"

The CPB or "Customer Perceived Benefit" is very different to the old USP (Unique Sales Point). Instead of focusing on what you think is a *sales* benefit to your clients, think about what the client will see to be a benefit *for them*. This means a bit more digging than before. What really matters to your clients? Put yourself in their shoes.

THOUGHT EXERCISE

Imagine you sell air conditioning.
What are your unique selling points? Perhaps your USP is offering delivery within 24 hours. Maybe you have an economical system that is cost-effective to install. Or perhaps your USP is that you provide the world's only range of purple air conditioners!

BUT... what if your client doesn't care about installation within 24 hours? What if your client actually wants to buy the top-of-the-range system, costing a fortune? What if (shock horror) your client doesn't actually want a purple aircon unit?

If you only focus on your USP, You may be investing in costly USPs that are completely unwanted. Fortunately, using the CPB approach, you may be able to both reduce your costs and sell more. The next step is to work through each of your target audiences, and then decide what they actually *want to hear* about your company, not just what you want to tell them.

Be realistic, be genuine, be honest and be positive!

Here is a list of example audiences and CPB-focused messages that are targeted to each audience:

Customers

EXAMPLE: We have listened to you and we understand that you want reliable deliveries and a courteous phone call to arrange an exact delivery time. If it looks like we won't meet that delivery slot, we will let you know immediately and arrange another time that suits you. We also know that you like us to minimise our packaging, and that you want to hear about our green credentials, so we've put packaging options as part of your ordering process. And our environmental policy is on our website - along with an invitation for you to submit your suggestions.

Staff

EXAMPLE: We are a great company to work with, our training scheme is second-to-none and you can earn far more working with us than with the competition. We are so well respected that having our company name on your CV can practically guarantee you a job anywhere in the world.
We are ahead of the game on technology and we have won awards for investing in our people and systems. Your colleagues are friendly and professional, we have great staff benefits.

Suppliers

EXAMPLE: We are fair to our suppliers. We pay on time, and we only put pressure on them when things are urgent. We communicate openly with them, and work in partnership with a number of suppliers which means we can offer new products.

Neighbours

EXAMPLE: We try to be good to our neighbours, we have policies about parking in allocated slots so we don't annoy them. We've found out what our neighbours' businesses do, so we can look out for business for them where possible, and we're arranging joint refuse collections to save us all money and help in our green policy.

Shareholders

EXAMPLE: We aim to be open and transparent for shareholders. We have frequent open days so they can come and talk to us about our business and find out more about our team. We have a shareholders' page on our website. We send them our business news at the same time as we send it to the press.

Distributors/agents

EXAMPLE: We offer full training for our agents and we have events for them to really get to know the company. We support them and fulfill promises they make to the best of our ability. We communicate openly with them and we're always keen to hear their feedback.

Others (eg: community, local government, MPs, trade associations, membership organisations, etc)

EXAMPLE: We hold open days for the community so they know about our business. We issue our press releases to the local press as well as the trade press, and we love to support community initiatives with products and prizes. We have meetings with the MP, and invite her to all our events. We are active in our trade associations and attend events whenever we can.

Competitors

EXAMPLE: Whilst we don't expect business from our competitors we do meet them at trade events, and we always ensure we are professional and polite. Sometimes this has led to collaborative work, but the very least it means they know about us and we know about them. In the event that we cannot fulfill an order we know which competitor to recommend.

You can see from the above responses that each sector has very specific interests. It's obvious that your customers don't care about your parking and your neighbours don't care one jot about your delivery schedule. This audience segregation is a useful exercise to undertake - it illustrates how dividing your audience into sectors makes it easier to communicate.

Step five - which communication method?

If you've worked through the past exercises, you've now got your messages, and you know who you want to tell them to. But how? Which are the best methods of communicating?

Identifying your communication methods

The answers to the "target audience" questions will help you identify who you are aiming your communications towards. Based on this, you can see what your target media is likely to be. Think about what media your audience will refer to in their business life.

Think, also, about what they read when relaxing. Business targets are also consumers in their own time.

Knickers to glossy mags!

I remember one of my clients saying that they only wanted to get stories about their company in trade magazines, despite the fact that they sold beautiful lingerie, which was widely available in most department stores.

It took me ages to convince them that we should also back up our PR with a good amount of consumer coverage in the glossy lifestyle titles.

It was this consumer coverage that really helped to create the greatest awareness for lots of reasons. Firstly these buyers were reading the magazines in their own time, and for enjoyment, not work. They had paid for the magazines themselves and were going to get every bit of value out of them.

The glossy magazines also had a decent budget for photoshoots, so our lingerie was being taken all round the world, from New York loft apartments to tropical beaches – and boy did it look good!

After my client had agreed that this was a good idea, I suggested taking it one step further and we started buying up quantities of these consumer magazines and posting them to the trade buyers "with our compliments" - what a nice, selfless gesture!!!

And the increased trade interest certainly showed how successful the campaign had been.

Lesson learned: the people we are communicating with are just that – people – and they have lives and interests outside of work.

Ask the Audience!

Unless you personally fall into one of the "target audience" categories, NEVER make assumptions about what the target audience reads, watches and listens to. Because the fact is, unless you have done your research you just don't know for sure!

I always think the best way to decide on a communication method is to ask the audience what they prefer. Consider doing a survey questionnaire or a focus group, to ask your targets what media they refer to.

NOTE: Even if you are one of the target audiences, still don't assume that you can answer for everyone; you still need to do some research!

Surveys

These can be as simple as a few phone calls to the relevant people, using an internet survey tool (there are several good ones, that are freely available) or you could invest in a mass-printed postal questionnaire campaign.

The actual people you are approaching will give you the key as to which to use. If your audience is a large group of consumers, and you don't have their email addresses, then a postal survey is likely to be the best option.

If the audience is a select group of senior directors, a phone call, or personal letter is likely to be better.

When you are doing this, consider the appropriateness of some sort of incentive for people to respond.

Focus Groups

A focus group is a gathering of people who come together to discuss something in a "focused" way, usually chaired by an independent chairperson. A focus group is likely to give you a lot more information than a simple questionnaire, as people will provide much useful information that you may never have considered.

This is also a great way of finding out about your CPBs or Client Perceived Benefits (see earlier: *"Step four - refine your key messages"*).

Often companies will run focus groups before they run a survey. The feedback they get from the focus groups are great for identifying new questions that need to be asked.

Many years ago my PR agency was appointed by a travel company who had previously been running BOGOF (Buy One Get One Free) promotions to students for years. Their promotions "two can travel for the price of one" had cost them many £thousands, but were not yielding the results they wanted.

Upon our appointment we suggested running focus groups to identify whether the promotion was as successful as it could be. Our focus group established something that no one had previously asked: students very rarely travel together on long distance journeys. If a student is studying in Edinburgh, and he chooses to go home to London, it is unlikely he will take his mates with him.

OUCH! Big money down the drain! Of course, after our focus groups we then had the information to turn it all around, but *you have to ask the audience to understand the audience.*

Getting the big picture

For a clear picture of what media is relevant to each sector, try evaluating for every target audience sector.

Here's an example evaluation, carried out for my lingerie client. We were targeting lingerie trade buyers, as you'll see! We also did some research with them, focus groups, surveys and general casual questioning, to build up an intelligent picture.

EXAMPLE
Target Audience: Professional Lingerie Buyers. (Professional buyers employed by department stores to select lingerie collections that the store will then sell to the public.)

Likely profile of person: Professional, male/female, under 65, over 18, experienced, understand retail, likely to have degree/further education.
Consider other things like: do they have children? Possible age? Leisure activities? Interests? What things concern them: stocks/shares, education, environment, politics, etc.

Magazines
At work: Womenswear, Drapers, Retail Week.

At home: Red, Harpers, FHM, Horse & Hound.

Newspapers
At work: FT, Telegraph.
At home: Local newspaper.

Internet sites
At work: Google, Magazine sites, Trade sites, Twitter, LinkedIn, competitor sites, fashion sites
At home: Yahoo, Facebook, Twitter, Google, news sites home shopping sites.

TV/Radio
News, relevant documentaries, personal choice on rest (not really relevant for this audience)

Target Media

Once you have the answers from your audience, you can consider your target media in general terms:

- Is it regional, national or even international?? How far does it spread?

- Business or consumer?

- TV? Ideal for something that is highly visual.

- Radio?   Do you have a good spokesperson? Interesting background noises?

- Newspapers? - local/regional, business-focused, community-led, what are their favourite topics?

- Online? - websites, blogs and digital media.

- Is your target media stable or changing frequently?

- Is it trade? And what sector of the trade?

- Are you aiming at distributors or end-users?

- Don't forget the media that your "influencers" read (see target audiences),

Many companies have lots of different media sectors, and the sectors will change according to the news available and the press releases required.

It's important to write for the sector - for example: your local newspaper doesn't want technical specifications, but your trade magazine probably will.

Other deciding factors

In getting out your message, there are other factors that you will need to take into account. To help you further identify the best routes to your target audience, ask yourself:

- Is your message time-sensitive?

- Is it vital that your message is published?

- Is your message essential information (e.g.: product recall)?

For all these, you need to consider:

- The media may not cover your article - they may have too much news already, or they may think yours is not important enough.

- The media may not publish the "vital" information that you need to get out.   Often the press will edit your release, to fit in with their space availability. This means you can lose out.

- Media deadlines may not coincide with your own. The media work to tight deadlines and it is rare for them to hold on just so they can print a press release!

- The media you choose has its own angles. For example, today's focus, for them, might be totally different from your "man makes millions" story, e.g. mums in work, or work/life balance.

- Consider how the media wants to receive your information. By email, a phone interview or even a video message. What if no-one is willing to give a phone interview or there isn't time to film a video?

If any of the above applies, you need to think about other ways to achieve your objectives. For example sending out a release with an "embargo", means that the media should* not publish it until your embargoed date. Work your way through the tools and activities chart to assess a suitable route.

*No guarantees though!

Putting it into practice

By now you're in an ideal position to write your first press release. You know your target audiences, your Customer Perceived Benefits, your sectors, your target media and what your influencers want to hear.

Just a simple matter then of putting fingertip to keyboard and bashing out a press release? And that's where the writers' block usually sets in. The very concept of having to be creative is enough to put most people off.

So, push your keyboard to one side for the moment and work your way through this list to help you on your way through the block - to the perfect release.

1. Go out and buy your local newspaper, or find your local, trade or business magazine.

2. Check out the internet, look for publications for user groups that may attract your target audience.

3. Read these media - in a different way:

- Look at the articles and decide what the hook was.

- Why are they interesting and how are they written?

- What sort of news gets into this media?

- Think about what would get your company into this media?

4. Complete the "Good News Exercise" (later in book).

5. Then, following our Press Release writing guide, write your release and mail it out!

Still got writer's block?

If it really isn't happening for you after all this, then just go do something different. There's no point in sitting at a blank screen beating yourself up emotionally. Take a walk. Grab a coffee. Do some other work that you enjoy. All this PR work you've been doing and reading about is now embedded in your mind, so your subconscious will carry on working on your press release whatever you're doing. And by the time you come back to work on it another day, it will probably flow.

TIP: By now, you are probably spotting stories and PR events in all the media you are reading. Create a "crib file" for inspiration - clip out articles, snippets, examples of writing techniques and things that interest you and store them in a file to refer to later.

Creative ideas for your press release

Always be on the look out for news; with a keen eye and a little creativity, you can create plenty of newsworthy stories - and you don't have to have a mega-budget. Once you start to look around you'll see there are more news-stories in your company than you ever thought possible.

Here are a few ideas for stories that can make the news. Perhaps they won't hit the national headlines, but you've every chance of getting into your local paper, community website or your trade magazine if the angle is right for them. Of course not all of these concepts are going to work for your organisation, but there should be at least three or four to get your juices flowing.

To be proactive in your PR campaign, watch out for stories evolving. If something falls into any of the categories in the list below, chances are it will be worthy of media attention. When any of these happen consider putting out a press release, writing it up on your website, putting it in your newsletter, sending out letters, calling a photocall, etc:

A brief word of warning: make sure that anything you do, you do for all the right reasons, not just to make the press. The media can sniff out "PR fluff" at 20 paces, and are very unlikely to cover anything that is blatant advertising or an empty PR stunt!

A New Product or Service

Now this sounds simple enough, but how often has your business introduced a new or improved product or service, without telling the press?

You only have to look at the amount of advertising budget that is given to a "new improved flavour of yoghurt" to realise that most new products could be big news! The key thing here is the *rationale* behind any improvements or new product/service launches.

Here you may need to go back to the drawing board and start asking people the reasons behind the changes. Have they done a customer survey? Are they responding to a change in the market? Will this improvement be greener, more environmental? Cost less to buy? Be more transportable…? Why why why? All the positive reasons behind the new or improved product/service need to be woven into your release.

New product alone, is not a story - but "new product that can save our customers ££££'s" - now that's great news.

The innovation behind the new product can be another part of your story. Remember to get information about how long it's taken to develop or research.

Get quotes from your directors, and from your customers, and put these into the press release.

If at all possible or appropriate, send the press a preview of the product before it is launched and let them try it out too. Their early involvement may add to your sales collateral if they give you a thumbs-up in print that you can also use in your brochures.

If you're launching a new book, remember the press deadlines and ensure that your book hasn't launched yet. The media are often happy to do previews and reviews of "just launched" - but bear in mind that this is "just launched" according to when *their* readers see the article. So if their print deadline is three months away, then they are unlikely to review a book that will be three months old by the time they go to press.

Consider revising your launch dates to fit the media - particularly if you have the luxury of flexibility with dates. If by moving your launch date a week or two, it means you get free media coverage, then would that be more beneficial for your business?

New products and product improvements are a great reason for making it a priority to stay in touch with everyone in your business. Popping in for a chat with the manufacturers, and keeping an eye on technology can pay dividends, if you can find out about a new product development in the future and plan this into your PR schedule.

New products and improvements are frequently relevant for both trade and local newspapers. If it is particularly visual or you've got some great interview opportunities or soundbites, try for radio and TV too.

Tip: A new product alone is not a story - but "new product that can save our customers ££££'s" - now that's great news.

Research

The press just love a research statistic. 9 out of 10 cats, 2 out of 3 headaches, etc. Think about what you want to get across to the newspapers, then think about how some statistics or research could back it up.

Focus on the people you'll be helping too - for example, if you make a product that appeals to parents, how about asking them how it makes their lives easier?

Of course research alone may not help you - you may need to be prepared to do some work behind the scenes to ensure it's pertinent to your business. For example, making those changes to deliveries, product or packaging.

Be mindful too: the press are intelligent. They are not going to use research that is in any way slanted or "massaged", they will want the true facts, and if that means using a third party to carry out the research then you'll need to factor that in.

A few years ago, I carried out a research project for a client. We had worked together for a long time, and did some pre-research brainstorming and questioning, so we already knew what the answers were likely to be, but the research had to be carried out to confirm our assumptions.

The research was for a major train company, and we wanted to find out about social interactions on the trains. We had anecdotal evidence (if you don't have this, then a focus group before the main research project can be excellent to point you in the right direction) and we used it to shape our questionnaires.

We then spent many hours on freezing station platforms around the country, asking people about their social interactions on the trains. Our target was to get 800 respondents, and we reviewed the responses frequently in case we didn't achieve our goals.

Finally, we hit the magic number of 800, and methodically analysed the results. Every questionnaire was stored and the full report created (to which the press had full access).

From this the press release: "Train travellers want to be more sociable" was born.

But even this wasn't going to be enough. The reason? We still had to *do* something about it. OK, so train travellers had spoken - overwhelmingly - and expressed how much they would like to talk more to their fellow commuters, but it was still a weak piece of PR without some action on behalf of our clients.

The answer: we created a booklet of "ideas for conversations", and we invited the media to accompany us when we gave these out free of charge on the trains. The booklets included a data-capture device supported by a competition, so we could use it to collect meaningful information for our client.

The uptake for the press release was excellent and we achieved national and local newspaper, TV news and radio coverage, with a number of celebrities continuing to use the material in their shows afterwards.

Yes, the project took a lot of work, but it was well worthwhile, resulting in many £'000's of media exposure and some excellent data for the train company.

NOTE: If you don't have time to do your own research, consider getting a third party to handle your research. This will add an extra element of endorsement and credibility.

A new appointment

Just employed the best salesperson in the industry? Did your new secretary have a past life as an Olympic pole-vaulter? Taken on someone who is an expert in their field? New appointments scream "success"!

New appointment releases are a great way of getting your name into the press, with a subliminal message (or maybe not so subliminal) saying: "We are growing, expanding, and employing more people"

If you've got a particularly interesting new team member, then getting a photograph of them indulging in their hobby (so long as it's appropriate and fits in with your company image) will be a useful asset. Of course, if you can really make a match between your business and your new member of staff (eg: your business makes ten-pin bowling balls, and your new recruit is a crown green champion) then that would be excellent. Links may be tenuous, but don't let that stop you trying.

New recruit photography can frequently be boring. Head and shoulder shots, against a white background - what a yawn! Aim to be a little different, do something that's appropriate and yet inspirational to photograph. Field Sales Manager? How about a shot of them, at their desk in a field? You get the picture.

Step outside the norm and get a great photo, and some interesting background and you'll be far more likely to achieve media coverage.

Think about the media who are most likely to be interested in this. Maybe your local newspaper will be good. Perhaps the local newspaper of the person you've employed. Trade press almost definitely!

Need to employ?

If you need to employ someone with specific or unusual skills, or if you are expanding apace, then this can be news! Both trade media and local news may be interested. As a press release item, this doesn't work every time, but it has certainly worked for me in the past. It's also saved me money having to pay for recruitment advertisements.

Of course if your vacancy is particularly unusual - think Lighthouse Manager, Lion Tamer or Pop Star - then you could be looking at a national news piece.

Unusual vacancies aren't just different in name only, the vacancy itself could offer a unique training opportunity, overseas travel to exotic destinations, or come complete with a great employment bonus, like living accommodation on a desert island. All of these are excellent hooks on which to hang a story, and they can even be great photo-opportunities to bolt into your press release.

If you are going to use a recruitment agency, have a chat with them to encourage them to maximise this opportunity for press for both of you.

I have often managed to get press coverage on the "need to employ" angle which have not only generated a great amount of interested candidates, the coverage also underpinned the overall success of the company.

New Premises

Unless you have down-sized, or moved your business into your garden shed, chances are that new premises could be of media interest.

Your new landlords will surely be delighted to get some coverage promoting their premises, so speak to them about their contribution towards the press release - for example, would they cover the cost of a photographer if they can use the photos afterwards?

In terms of the press, think local, trade and possibly also the estate's newsletters. If your new building has some unusual features, a historic past or a total refurbishment, then don't forget to mention this too!

If your business or premises are prestigious or unusual enough then you can consider asking a celebrity or local figure to come along to the official opening. Be imaginative about this photo opportunity: key presentations or cutting a ribbon across the door, is boring... but a giant ribbon that goes all the way around the building - now that can make a great photograph!

Often new premises can be a great excuse to hold an open day, so use this newsworthy item to publicise your amazing open event, charitable involvement or special offers.

A BIG order!

This may be more appropriate for B2B companies, but it will depend on what you've sold. A major land sale may work for the local media, but a massive business order is definitely one for your trade press too. Always remember your local press, especially if this order or commission will mean more wealth and jobs coming into the area.

For trade, be prepared to disclose the financial aspects of the deal, and be prepared to disclose details of the customer. Often a customer quote in the release will make for good reading.

This sort of release is excellent to get across the CPBs (Customer Perceived Benefits) of your products and company, and they can be woven into the story - e.g. "client X said "I much prefer …"

A renewed contract is not quite as newsworthy, but don't dismiss it entirely, particularly in a tough economy.

A new approach to a market

Decided to make everything in the UK instead of abroad? Outsourcing to a firm of workers with disabilities? Decided that distributors will be more effective than agents? Changed manufacturing techniques to cut carbon footprint?

Depending on the size and scale of your business change, these could be mainly a story for the trade press... or they could go national.

But whatever the size of your changes, this is news that can lead to a great corporate profile exercise for you. This is the sort of news story that will either be a tiny snippet or a lengthy article.

NOTE: As with all stories, consider whether or not there are negative impacts from your story. If so, be very careful with releasing the information to the press.

Something that makes a difference to someone's life

How the media will lap this up! Nothing better than a human-interest story. If your product or company has helped someone – in a medium-to-major way, then tell people about it!

A few examples

- Your product eases pain and suffering.
- Your service/product now means that Mrs. Bloggs can get her pension with less hassle.
- Your new pet food range supports a donation to a third world charity.
- You're inspiring people with disabilities by employing someone with the same disability.
- Your product helps a schoolchild to do their homework...

This sort of news story can really spread. Of course you've got the local media, but you've also got the trade press, and potentially the nationals.

Note: if the people you are helping are vulnerable, ensure they are adequately represented and that they are quoted correctly. Most important: ensure that difference you are making is genuine, appropriate, sizeable and sustainable.

Charitable affair

From hosting a charity ball, to sponsoring a staff swimathon, donating the shirts to the local youth football team, or donating staff time to help renovate a hostel for the homeless. If you aren't currently doing anything, then consider suggesting it to your employees. Charitable involvement is great for staff morale and, of course, for the press.

Try to link the charitable event with your product or service. If you make paint, then donate both paint and people to a charity to "make a difference".

Human interest story

Human interest is always high on the local press agenda. If your business is supporting a worker in achieving their life's ambitions, perhaps helping them to trek round the world, or to do an MBA, then your company and its people, deserve the attention of the media.

Don't hide your light, get that release out!

Accompany this story with a great photo. Or, if appropriate, offer journalists a photocall opportunity - but remember costs and time constraints means that they may not turn up, so sending a photograph with your release will be safer.

Successful completion of contract or project

Done a good job for someone? Then tell the press about it. If the client was a blue-chip organisation, a charity, not-for-profit, or local, there's every chance that the national press will be interested.

Of course even better is for the customer to tell the press for you - you do this by making sure the client approves the press release and preferably gets their quote in it too.

Photographs for this sort of release would typically include the smiling client, the smiling client account manager, and a picture of the project/product.

Relevant media, depend on the contract or project's scope and target audience. Local, trade, national… all are potentially interested.

Another bonus for this close client work is that you get the client endorsement as a testimonial. It's been approved for the public domain, so using it on your website (ask for their permission first out of courtesy) can be another excellent sales tool.

Controversial or outspoken opinion?

Something going on in your industry, town or environment that you have a controversial, valued or expert opinion about?

You can either issue a press statement, a press release, send a letter to the editor or just pick up the phone. Once you become known for being outspoken, the media may start to call you for a comment.

For this reason alone, it is good to have a stock file of photographs of key spokespeople.

Expert Opinion

So you or your staff are experts? Know all there is to know about VAT or climate change or IT or purple chickens? Then consider: would your local press or trade press be interested in you writing a column?

Issuing a simple how to guide can generate media coverage. Or how about a whole series of "how to" guides?

Such guides underpin your position as an expert, and give people a feeling of bonhomie. "How to" guides are probably more trade or business-orientated than local press, but it does depend on your product.

Even if you have a product or service that is quite unusual, ask your clients "what element of your knowledge would they find useful"?

Get started by writing an example column, a few paragraphs or even just a brief synopsis. Then speak to your media to find out what they think.

The launch of your own book will fully endorse you as an expert, and the media are more likely to focus on the book - using excerpts from it. Of course, every time the media promote your book they are promoting you, so start thinking about writing.

More and more people are writing blogs, and using these to house your expert knowledge can help to separate "selling website" from "expert blog", thus encouraging the media to pay you a little more attention. The really good news here is that people now subscribe to blogs through Kindles and e-readers much the same way as they would a magazine, so your reach can be that much wider.

Birthdays and anniversaries

Whether your company has just made it to 12 months, or 120 years, an anniversary is cause for celebration. Mark the milestones in your company's history by letting the press know.

Boost coverage by doing something memorable on the event, from having a giant birthday cake, to launching a fund-raiser or giving something to charity.

Add some more interest to your celebration using creativity - invite a celebrity, give away a number of limited edition products, perhaps get an artist to create a commemorative sculpture, or reprint your first ever company brochure, sixties hairstyles 'n' all!

Event

You can host an event for many reasons. But unless you want to keep it to a quiet soiree it is worth informing the press. Bear in mind that you may not want to invite everyone to your event, and by going public beforehand, you are almost obliged to ensure that everyone is invited.

Post-event releases, including photographs of attendees or memorable moments in the event, are probably most likely to find their way into the local Chamber of Commerce magazine and website. Remember to send the press release and photos out to your clients and contacts who attended. They may be able to put them on their own business website, thus building another valuable link and promotion to yours.

Consider using your event to generate funds for your charity or to support and promote the ethos of the charity. You can do this by inviting charity representatives to speak, taking the pressure off you!

A post-event release can be just as successful as a pre-event release, with the added bonus that you can include client comments, great photographs and quotes.

"Most-est"

I love those three little letters: E S T. If you can add them to any word, you've probably got a news story. Is yours the biggest, brightest, newest, fastest, slowest? If your product or service is the "most" of anything, then that could be news.

Turn to any news source, pick up almost any magazine or newspaper and you'll be sure to find at least one example of "est".

Using the EST test, you absolutely must put it into focus - a simple check is to always add two statements;
1) the rationale behind the EST claim, e.g. we're the most used toilet paper, because surveys say more people buy our brand.
2) the reasons you've been able to make your 'EST claim', e.g. people say they buy our toilet paper because we are more environmentally friendly and they say our product is softer.

Without these reinforcing statements, which should ideally be from a third party, your EST statement may be seen by the media as pure fluff and relegated to the file marked "bin".

Of course there may be other EST claims for which you refer to historical or documented facts, e.g. "we're moving into the oldest building in the town". And whatever you claim under the EST rule, remember to substantiate and back it up. Then, by using the reasoning behind the EST, you can weave in your key messages, e.g. "we chose the oldest building in town because our company's products are designed for longevity, with many lasting over 50 years."

Great photograph

Maybe your story line isn't too strong, but the photo will be amazing.

The media loves great photography. Often a fantastic photo can transform an otherwise dull (and un-newsworthy) story into a headliner. But never try to make a weak story look exciting by padding out the release, instead just do a short release/caption and mail out the photo.

There are two ways of maximising a headline-grabbing photograph opportunity:

1) Arrange a photocall - invite the press to take the shot.
2) Take it yourself/book a photographer.

If you take the first option, always remember the press photographer may not show up, so make sure you've got your own photographer on hand too.

The big no-no!

When you produce a new brochure – do you expect the press to write a news article about it? When you get a new phone line installed, do you immediately rush to telephone your local news desk? No!

Then, please treat your website in exactly the same way. The Internet is just a tool, like a phone line. Your website* is really a back-lit brochure and customer-engagement tool. Unless your site provides a really innovative solution and is an interesting place to be (and I mean *really*) then don't even think of releasing it to the press as a stand-alone press release! Such releases are viewed with as much scorn as an invitation to the opening of an envelope!

Yes, of course you should publicise your site in every way possible including putting your url onto every release, but to issue a press release purely on a new brochure-style website stopped being newsworthy when the 5-millionth website was launched in the '90s.

* I'm talking about the website itself, not the amazing tools it may contain. These tools themselves, may well be worthy of a release.

Getting a grip on creativity

As you'll have seen from the preceding suggestions, there are so many opportunities to create news stories for your business that I challenge any organisation that claims it has no news.

So, how do you go about using all your amazing ideas, and still getting your day job done? I suggest you create an annual schedule of events and creative suggestions. Certain events, like Christmas, come once a year, so put them straight into your schedule. Then look at media deadlines to issue releases - and incorporate those into your schedule too.

See below for a basic outline. I find planning invaluable when it comes to getting an overview of activities and spacing things out well.

Activity	Idea	Jan	Feb	Mar....
Valentines promotion	10% off if you bring your partner	Issue press release	Hold event 14/2	Post-event release
Open Day	Business is 10 years old	Invite MP	Issue release	Hold event 26/3
Easter Promotion	Low key - ref 10 year anniversary			Mail eggs. No PR

"So what?"

By now you've probably thought of lots of times when you could have sent out a release, but have decided it wasn't newsworthy enough. One way to do a quick reality-check on whether your release idea is likely to work is to ask yourself the "so what" question.

Put yourself in the mindset of one of the readers, listeners or viewers of your chosen media. Does your press release idea answer the "so what?" question for them? Does it: inform, educate, entertain, amuse, surprise, sadden, worry, concern, or generate the emotion/action you want?

If it has the potential to elicit any of these emotions, go right ahead. If not, bin your idea and start again.

Writing the news story

Now you have a clearer idea of what is likely to make the news it's time to get writing a release.

The following tool is very useful to ensure you have remembered everything (especially when it comes to getting quotes approved by company representatives).

Try using it for your first 3 or 4 releases until you get used to the format.

1) Date.

2) Details of what you sell - products you offer/services you provide.

3) Story: (Remember "What makes news?")

4) Reason for interest: consider your audience; why should they read this story? Have you covered the "So What" factor?

5) Why should a journalist cover this story? Is it topical, relevant, newsworthy, does it appeal to the readership?

6) Supporting information: case studies, quotes, statistics.

7) What messages do you think the story conveys?
- Are there other messages you would like to convey?
- Is it possible to weave them into this story? How?

9) Negative messages you may be portraying
- how can they be removed/minimised?

10) Time sensitivity. Does this news need to be released by a certain date?

11) Who does this story appeal to?

- Trade press.
- Consumer media.
- National.
- Local.
- Regional.
- Internet/blogs/online magazines/news media
- TV. Is it a visual experience?
- Radio. Is it an audio experience? Are there suitable background noises available?

12) Are there photographs available or can you set up a photocall?

13) If photocall – when, where, how?   Put information into press release.

14) Have you included a quote in this release? Did the person quoted approve the quote? Do you have proof that they signed off their quote as approved for press release use?

Transforming the questions into a press release

With the information from the previous exercise you should be ready to turn this into a press release. You can develop your own format for a release, but here is a suggested format to kick off:

1) Date – at the top of the page

2) **Heading** – in LARGE BOLD PRINT (not underlined).

3) First paragraph (include: who, what, when, why and where). No longer than 50-60 words.

4) More paragraphs. Just four or five more of INTERESTING information!

5) A quote from someone relevant or important (e.g. MD of the company/client company).

6) Add your website url into the last paragraph if at all possible.

7) Type **"/ends"** To show there is no more to follow.

Remember – shorter is better. Your press release should be no longer than two A4 pages, preferably only one. If it ends up longer, then don't decrease font size – try to edit as much as possible. If you don't edit – the journalist surely will.

8) "Editor's Notes" As a second page. General information about your company. Almost like the "about page" on your website

Once the "editor's notes" are written they will often stay the same for each release, so long as they are still applicable.

Here is a suggested format for "editor's notes":

EDITORS NOTES
Contact Details:

- Who issued release?   (Name, company, contact details)
- Who can be quoted, whom can the press call for more information? "For further information contact: _____ (your details, address, telephone, website, email, etc."
Ensure the contacts you name WILL be available to respond!

BACKGROUNDER *
2 or 3 short paragraphs about your company.

When were you established?
What do you do?
Who do you do it to/for?
What claims to fame do you have (if any)
Where are you based?
Your website url and other appropriate urls.

*The backgrounder has a good chance of being published, so write it well, with a view to how it may appear in the press.

NOTE: Remember to make your press release "key word rich", so for online media it can also serve to boost your own website rankings and the chance of people finding your company.

The press release – golden rules

Media releases (or press releases) are powerful and cost-effective tools. But there are a few golden rules that must be observed.

- Never send out a media release that isn't newsworthy; it will just start to irritate and alienate the press and your next release may end up in the bin before they have even looked at it. Now is the time to start building up your reputation with the press as a company that issues interesting news stories. So make sure you have read the media, you understand what they print, and you know what they perceive is news to their readers.

- Make sure your release is relevant to that media. Sometimes you'll need to prepare several versions of one release to make sure it appeals to each media sector.

- Work up a catchy heading. But nothing too clever or obscure.

- Follow the standard format. Keeping to the format means you will keep it brief, but you won't miss out important information.

- Pack your release full of keywords and phrases. Remember to include your url and/or landing pages. This will help you gain more visits to your website and help your release get found online. Check with your web experts which keywords are best.

- Consider the best way to send it out. Email? Post? If in doubt, ask the journalist you are sending it to. If you're issuing by email then put the release into the body of the email - journalists often refuse to open attachments.

- Accompany your release with a good photograph. Not a dodgy one from your smartphone, but something you'd be proud to see in print. Check what the media requirements are for photographs, dpi, sizes, etc.

- Make sure it is addressed to the right person. Keep your database of contacts up to date.

- Check media deadlines/publication dates BEFORE you upload it to your website. This is a balancing act, you don't want to miss putting it online, but you really don't want to pre-empt journalists/media who may publish it.

- Include links to your website or blog. If you've referred to other sources also provide the links and information for journalists to find easily.

The Power of Media Relations

It has long been widely accepted that PR coverage is three times more valuable than advertising, however this figure fluctuates, so Google "advertising v PR" for the latest stats.

Reliable surveys of how readers see ads/editorial are quite thin on the ground, but this one was very useful:

In a survey 69% of readers said they see advertisements in a magazine as a source of information. However, a massive 81% of readers said that an editorial recommendation in a magazine is more likely to make them try a product.

The research also shows that consumers display a strong bond with their chosen publication/magazine and spend a great deal of time reading it. They return time and time again to it reaping ideas and believe what they read in the editorial sections.

An advertorial can educate and provide detailed product benefits to the reader. It is considered value-added advertising and gives the perceived joint control of advertiser and editor therefore giving a strong implied endorsement. The media's brand values feed the advertorial and influence the brand and product perception. 1

1 Source: National Magazine Company 2000

Q: What Turns a Journalist On?

A: "It's for you…"

A few years ago I did a piece of research for a training course I was running. I wanted to show the delegates just how diverse journalists are in what they like and dislike. It raised a few laughs and a lot of eyebrows.

I think it illustrates perfectly that the one size fits all approach does not work as well as a more tailored "it's for you" approach.

The answers were given to the question: "What turns you on – what do you look for from a press release"?

The course I was running was for the IT industry, so there is a bias towards IT and business in the answers, but from experience I can assure you that this applies across the board. The answers have been printed exactly as they were given.

Journalist from a national daily broadsheet.

"If you're looking for coverage it must be about listed companies, BT, Orange, etc. Our readers tend to be educated shareholders. They don't want boring techie stories. They refer to us for entertainment, information, and to find out about investments, shares etc.

"The majority of our stories come from stock exchange announcements.

"And, if a company is not listed we don't print the story. Unless it is a VERY good story- or an exclusive."

SUMMARY: Make releases relevant, and write them as though you know the media you are sending them to.

Journalist & contributor to a national daily broadsheet, a management magazine and a Sunday newspaper.

"Newsworthiness. Something useful. "A computer company is going to make a computer" is NOT news. "No set formula, though, whatever is the flavour of the week. I tend to write about things that make a difference to SMEs. Case studies are always the best though. Real life examples of things that make a difference. For example: Software that saves time, and an example of a company that is using it.

"Photos help. But never send a large attachment.

"I keep things on file for a long time. Clients may get a call five or six months after sending me a press

release. Following up on a release sometimes helps as it jogs my memory."

SUMMARY: Focus on current issues. Never give up hope. If something isn't printed immediately it may resurface in a few months.

Editor, IT Business Magazine, monthly.

"What will get in? An issue that is important to our readership. Is a product launch going to be interesting. No! Is a piece of software interesting. No! I want to examine real issues that people are dealing with. Or solutions that have not been done before. Like recycling, late payments, etc. What's happening in the Channel is currently very interesting to us. But blatant product promotions just don't cut it here. Any journalist with three months experience can see through PR fluff.

"If you are going to come and talk with me, then come in with several different ideas. Don't just come in with one thing. If that's not interesting, the conversation will stop there. I'd rather have a rambling conversation with someone and out of that I'll pick up the things that are important.

"We never take case studies and we never take by-lined articles. Product shots are a waste of time. We do NOT use them. We will use head and shoulder portraits if the person looks particularly odd. Interesting pics of people doing interesting things are better."

SUMMARY: Avoid flannel, less fluff, more candid honesty. Consider speaking with a journalist on issues (but make sure you don't drop yourself in it. i.e.: Don't talk to a journo about having cash flow problems in your company- the next thing you might read about is your plummeting share prices!)

Journalist, IT and business magazine

"We like to publish industry-wide findings, research. Not company research or just product releases.

"We also like to publish order signings. If you've got a good order signing that will usually make it in.

"One of the best ways of getting into the magazine is by making a suggestion for an interesting feature.

"Photos are always good, especially unusual photos not just head and shoulder portraits.

"One thing that is annoying is if people send information that we have said we don't want. For example an order signing with no price on the order."

SUMMARY: Listen to exactly what the journalist wants – to the letter. Suggestions on features are useful.

Contributor to a number of IT and business magazines

"Don't ever say you have a customer but you can't say who it is! It drives us mad! In a case study you

must name the people. We don't want to know all about the technical side of things, like how its made, we want to know how it makes a difference to your customers.

"We appreciate meals and drinks etc, but it's not going to buy your story in. What it will do, though, is mean we are more likely to remember you for what you do . . . when we come to cover it.

"Don't embargo anything for more than 3 days. Some companies have a launch and then embargo things for up to three months. Who's going to remember that?

"Don't go to the press if you're going to be difficult about the content of your story and not provide all the information and details. We just get frustrated and we won't call you in the future.

"If you have a presentation or press launch – keep it short. Leave the technical bits out. If people want to know, they can ask you later!

"On ring-round features, stick to the time allocated. If you say you'll call me at 4pm, then call me at 4pm!

"Don't ask me for a list of questions before an interview. I want to talk generally- not specifically."

Summary: Make sure you can refer to your customers in case studies. Stick to what you promise. Don't embargo anything for more than a few days – if at all.

Senior journalist, IT magazine, monthly

"We are only interested in customer stories, we have no use for product stories unless a major company is bringing out a huge revolutionary new system.

"Have no interest in IT sector customers, only big names but we do like to use case studies.

SUMMARY: When talking to this title, make sure it's about people, not products, case studies are fine but unless it's a product by the big five they're unlikely to be interested.

Editor, technical and business magazine

"I will always be much more receptive to PR companies that have read the magazine. They need to understand the magazine, what we're interested in is obvious if you read the publication, we don't have the time to reel off lists of what we accept and what we don't.

"You could send us the most fantastic press release ever written, but if you haven't researched and targeted the correct publications no one is ever going to see it."

SUMMARY: Researching the publication really pays off.

Senior Reporter, IT weekly magazine

"I would like it if PROs could be up to speed on campaigns we are running, also that they know what I write about and what I'm interested in is important.

"A good in-depth knowledge of their clients and their clients business is essential, so they can answer questions quickly and astutely.

"Also advance diary notice of up and coming events rather than a phone call two hours before the event starts.

"I much prefer to get to the heart of the story straight away. I really dislike being chased about a story, and if I haven't contacted you about its unlikely I'm using it."

SUMMARY: Be aware of what campaigns the magazine is running so that you can feed relevant information, do your homework on the magazine and the company you represent.

Editor, business IT magazine, monthly

"When we are invited to events there needs to be a purpose for them, if the only reason for us being there is for the PR companies to score brownie points with their clients, then the next time we are invited along to something, we are much less likely to attend.

"My main difficulties with press releases are the cold calls to ask if I received the release, and will it be used. These are frustrating and waste my time, if I'm interested I'll call you!

"PR companies need to do more research into the publications their sending the press releases to. PRs should start using a more targeted approach, calling ahead to ask about up and coming features or even requesting a features list is a much more constructive route to take.

"I'm happy to accept case studies and technical articles, but no educational stuff, we also experience a lot of pressure about extensive branding on stories, which we are not happy to do".

SUMMARY: Always be sure to have a constructive reason if inviting a journalist to an event, don't waste their time, target your approach.

Editor, IT business magazine

"I would prefer a stronger focus on research into the magazine, we are constantly sent product announcements which are a complete waste of time and most of my other dislikes lead back to the fact that there seems to be little or no research done by PRs, if time was taken to find out what we cover regularly and what we don't, I'm sure both parties would benefit.

"I'm happy to receive press releases, but am unlikely to use them and follow up calls, are a complete waste of time. It is also imperative that when a PR is asked for information from a journalist they respond coherently and quickly to us.

"I find PR companies really come in to their own when they take on the role of middleman between client and journalist.

"PR's exist to get good coverage for their clients, therefore working in partnership with journalists should be high on their priority lists."

SUMMARY: A quick reaction to the task requested by the journalist is a first-rate way to build up good relationships.

Editor, manufacturing, business & logistics magazine, monthly

"I would like to receive a quarterly list of relevant clients with a profile of their company, that will allow me to see if there is a few I can focus on, and therefore build up a relationship with.

"The majority of people that work in the media industry will be aware that monthly publications work quite far in advance and therefore would prefer to be contacted two to three months in advance. That would certainly be preferable to the day before the event took place.

"Press releases are fine but we are looking at a move to coding all mail so it can be slotted into relevant categories as it comes through.

"Timewasting is frustrating. It is all well and good being invited out to a fantastic resturant or hotel, but if there's no valid reason don't invite us! ! ! !

"I am always impressed when a PR company rings us for a features list and then offers a contribution to the magazine, the company has done their homework, they are much more likely to be contacted again."

Summary: Build up long-term relationships based on trust and respect. Being focused is vital.

A few example releases

As you'll have seen from the previous chapter journalists all want different things from a press release. But the basic premise is research: knowing the media inside out.

All the following releases were written and despatched to the media. They were "tweaked" and changed as required by the various journalists and editors. For example a release that is to go to the regional press may start off by pointing out that the company is based in their location. The same release when sent to the trade press, may not even mention the location of the company as it is just not important.

As a result, one PR campaign can generate more than four or five releases – all about the same thing, but all with a different slant, a different photo and a different quote from a different person. E.g. trade media may prefer a company spokesperson, but a regional newspaper may prefer a local resident.

These releases, therefore, simply show how a release can be formulated, how the story unfolds, and how the journalist will normally receive information.

All the following releases received coverage, some in the local press; others went as wide as national TV and radio.

NOTE: Some of these releases have had a few details changed, this is just to clarify how a press release can work and the factors you'll need to consider.

MEDIA RELEASE
Issued DD/MM/YYYY for immediate use

"Two pints of lager and a cholesterol test, please!"

Men in a Newtown pub may get a little more than they bargained for at lunchtime on Friday 18th June, when they will be offered a free men's health check with their usual tipple.

Members of the community organisation, Community Counts, have enlisted the help of local healthcare and fitness professionals to offer information and health advice to the customers of the White Horse Pub in Newtown.

Sarah Smith, manager of the Community Counts organisation, said: "Everyone is shocked to learn that the life expectancy of men in the Newtown area is 6 years lower than the national average. Part of our aim is to address this terrible statistic, and improve the quality of life and health for all our residents.

"One way we can achieve this is by helping people understand and take care of their health.

Rather than sit back and wait for people to come to find her, Sarah and her team decided on the unusual approach of taking the message to the people.

"Whilst people will visit the doctors if they are ill, they are often less interested in prevention and positive health action, so it was important that we went out to meet people and engage with them on their terms.

"Friday lunchtimes at The Whitehorse Pub usually tend to be fairly busy so it seemed like an ideal place to be"

From 11:30 to 2pm at The Whitehorse, residents, customers and interested parties, will be able to get a cholesterol check, blood pressure reading, height and weight checks, advice on healthy eating and even try out an exercise bike!

People will also be able to get specialist advice from the local dietician, Alcohol and Drug Programme (ADP) and find out about other events in the area.

"We are aiming to make this a fun and informative event," said Sarah. "If it goes well, we would consider making it a regular event".

John Smith, Manager of the White Horse Public House said: "I am keen to do my bit to help improve the health and fitness of people in the area. After all, I live here and have many friends here and I don't want us to become statistics!"

The event will take place (time/date/venue) Everyone will be welcome to come along and get a comprehensive health check and advice.
ENDS

Editors Notes

Release issued by Sue Haswell, Big Results, www.bigresults.co.uk
Tel: 01626 864458
Email; sue.h@bigresults.co.uk

(NOTE: With this release, I was the only contact provided so the press needed to contact me for more information).

BACKGROUND

Community Counts is a community-led initiative aimed at improving neglected and disadvantaged local communities.

Using funding from local government, communities and agencies have been working together to decide how this money will be best used to regenerate the community by creating real employment and training opportunities, better housing, a healthier quality of life, safer communities, a cleaner environment and improvements in educational achievement.

Office workers' stress costing UK business £1.5bn a day!

Office workers' stress and personal "downtime" could be costing British Business around £1.5bn a day, according to a survey commissioned by a leading computing company, Compass Computers Ltd, of Worcestershire.

The survey, based on telephone interviews with over 2000 office workers, was intended to identify the impact IT failures have on stress. It showed that over 56% of employees get stressed when IT fails – a key issue in today's stress-focused workplace. It also showed, that the cost of this stress amounted to some £1.5bn per day. *

The research also illuminated several other worrying trends:
- On average, each employee spends one hour and forty three minutes each day fixing IT issues.
- 97% of the employees asked rely on IT for their work. 62% of these said they spend time sorting out failed IT, 34% said they spend more than a quarter of their time fixing IT issues and a massive 21% of employees say they spend ALL of their time sorting out errant systems.

- Another concern is that when an IT problem reared its head, 26% of workers were relying on manuals, guessing or "not knowing at all". Only 31% would phone technical support and 23% rely on "experience" when handling IT problems.

Compass Computers' MD, Martyn West said: "These findings are extremely worrying. We know that people are stressed and lose productivity when IT fails them, but this actually identifies by how much. It is costing companies a lot of money, when there are alternative solutions available."

"Ongoing training, friendly telephone support and service response agreements could all help save stress and pounds", said Martyn West. "All of these can be done by Compass Computers or any reputable IT company"

Amazingly (or maybe not so amazingly) Compass Computers can come to the rescue with other issues too: "We offer a full systems review" said Martyn West, "working through everything the client needs in plain, non-jargon English.   We also provide on-site technical support for the duration of all our installations, ensuring that everything is running 100% smoothly before we leave clients to their own devices".

And if that's not enough good news for stressed-out office workers, Compass Computers have also come to the rescue with a laughter-filled "Stress Buster" download at www.compasscomputers.co.uk

Martyn West said: "It's well known that laughter is the best medicine, so we will keep the Stress Buster offer open until everyone has switched over to using Compass Computers."

* Source: Analysis, 2004,
/ENDS

Editors Notes
Survey: Jan/Feb/Mar 2003. Survey Analysis available. Please contact sue.h@bigresults.co.uk

For further information contact:
Martyn West, MD, Compass Computers
Tel: 0123 4567890
Email: **mw@compasscomputers.co.uk**

Release issued by Sue Haswell, Big Results, www.bigresults.co.uk
Tel: 01626 864458
Email; sue.h@bigresults.co.uk

About Compass Computers

Compass Computers, are specialists in designing, building and installing, PCs and networks, telecoms and software.

Established in 1999, Compass Computers' philosophy is about total business support. The company's teams of experienced and friendly engineers, work with clients to assess their needs, and ensure that they are met for the long-term success of each individual business. Compass' continued pursuit of technical excellence has ensured successful implementations for many larger companies across the UK.

Birmingham restaurant hosts a first

Birmingham is set to host the first "Power Networking" event in the UK at Lasan Restaurant, St Paul's Square, on Friday 3rd September.

"Power Networking" is the brainchild of Lasan's Director, Jabbar Khan, and is based loosely on the increasingly popular speed dating concept, but applied to the business world to promote a fun but productive networking environment.

With the success of his award-winning restaurant, Jabbar is tipped to be one of the main influencers in Birmingham business. "I attend many networking events, and really rate networking as a key way to do business." Jabbar said. "However one of the bugbears about networking is that often you only get to meet a few people at an event, and there are sometimes awkward situations where you get caught in a discussion and you can't get away.

"Power Networking is designed be full-on, unashamed, no-excuses networking."

Lasan Restaurant, has scooped several prestigious awards and listings including: Top 10 restaurants (Independent) and featured in Good Food Guide 2004 and Time Out. It is also acclaimed to be "one of the best Birmingham restaurants" by Paul Fulford, Evening Mail, "great Indian food" by The Guardian, and given four stars by The Birmingham Post.

Now, having won the hearts and taste buds of Birmingham's social diners, Lasan's innovative and pioneering concept is set to make waves in the business community. Jabbar continued: "we already serve many of Birmingham's movers and shakers, including hosting their client entertainment and corporate events. This will be a first for Lasan and, we believe, for Birmingham."
/ENDS

Editors Notes
For more information on the Power Networking Event, contact issuer below.

Press Release issued by:
Release issued by Sue Haswell, Big Results,
www.bigresults.co.uk
Tel: 01626 864458
Email: sue.h@bigresults.co.uk

About Lasan Restaurant

Lasan Restaurant is at the cutting edge of gourmet-eating, Indian style. It offers the very latest in menu innovation, interior design and sensory indulgences. Customers, food critics, and industry experts alike, have been extremely impressed. In fact they believe Lasan is contributing to Birmingham's growing reputation as a centre of excellence for dining out in style.

Have a free mental workout at stately 'Open House'

Birmingham's Woodbourne Priory Hospital is opening its doors to the public for the first time with a weeklong series of free mental strength seminars, from Monday 7th to Friday 11th October.

To coincide with World Mental Health Day on 10th October, the Woodbourne Priory is inviting people to its "Open House for Open Minds: A week to build mental strength", at it's tranquil and stately residence in Edgbaston, Birmingham.

Aimed primarily at the friends and families of those who are or may be suffering from mental health problems, the seminars will provide essential support and advice to those who play a vital role in the recovery and care of patients.

Visitors will be encouraged to learn about mental health issues, how they can affect us, and will be given advice on coping strategies, as well as valuable information on the support and treatment that is available.

Each evening throughout the week will cover a different topic:

Mon 7th - Understanding Post-Natal Depression.
Tues 8th - Overcoming Addiction.
Weds 9th - Recovering from Eating Disorders.
Thurs 10th - Combating Depression.
Fri 11th - Stress Management.

If you have friends or family that may be suffering from any mental health problems, or you yourself would like to learn more about any of the topics being discussed, then please call The Woodbourne Priory Hospital on 0123 456 7890, to reserve your free place at this extremely worthwhile event.
/ENDS
Editors Notes

Release issued by Sue Haswell, Big Results, www.bigresults.co.uk
Tel: 01626 864458
Email; sue.h@bigresults.co.uk

About the Woodbourne Priory Hospital
Priory Healthcare is the leading independent provider of specialist mental healthcare and includes addiction treatment, child and adolescent services, the care of people with eating disorders and general psychiatry.

Priory operates 17 acute psychiatric hospitals and units across the UK, two dedicated rehabilitation hospitals offering specialist brain injury and stroke rehabilitation services and a number of other smaller rehabilitation units.

After the release

CONGRATULATIONS!!! You've slaved hours over a beautiful piece of prose, toiled with dictionary and thesaurus to create something Shakespeare would have been proud of. And now, after many nail biting minutes staring at your PC screen, wondering if it can be improved, and you're about to blind-copy it to the perfect list of journalists and editors… (well, you don't want all the journalists knowing it's gone to their mates too!)

… or are you?

I mean, once you hit the "send" button - what next? Do you simply trust to chance, hoping the release will have been picked by a journalist to be their lead story of the day? Or do you now pick up the phone and try to help attract attention to your news-breaking story?

Some people will caution you against phoning journalists, some will encourage you. I say it's entirely up to you. Often a quick phone call can get a journalist to consider your idea, or to drag out the release that had been previously relegated to the bottom of the pile. If you are going to phone around, then I suggest you follow these guidelines.

- Journalists are very busy people, so be brief and get to the point.

- NEVER call them up to say "have you used my release?" If it is important to you that they have used it, then you should be buying their publication and reading it!

- Consider calling *before* you send the release so you can discuss a potential angle or idea you may have. Pre-pitching the release can make it seem so much more exclusive to them... and of course, any ideas you discuss can be reiterated in the follow-up email as a reminder.

- It is not the journalist's job to send you copies of what they have printed. If you get a friendly journalist who does this, then rejoice and work hard to build the relationship.

- One favourite follow-up technique is to call up the journalists saying there are new photos available and ask them what format would they prefer.

- Ask the journalist what they would like in future. How do they prefer to receive releases? How do they prefer to receive photos?

- Think hard about what you say. The best rule is - if you don't want it printed… DO NOT SAY IT!

- Often a journalist or editor will be too busy to sit and chat with you, but if you do speak to one who is happy to have a conversation, make the most of it. Pick their brains; find out what they are interested in from a journalistic perspective. Such relationships can be very rewarding.

When a journalist calls you

When a journalist calls you it is ALWAYS good news. Whether they are trying to find out more about your company, or sniff out a bad story, at least they are calling you – so you get the opportunity to maximise the positive and minimise the negative.

Here are a few useful rules for dealing with a phone call from the media:

- "No comment" = "guilty as charged." Never say "no comment" even if you genuinely don't have one. Ask the journalist what question they would like answering, then promise to phone them back with the answers. And make sure you keep your promise.

- If you do not have the answers, then get them! Formulate your comments, write them down, then call back to the journalist to read out your beautifully scripted response. Do not be drawn on these comments unless you are entirely comfortable.

- There is no such thing as "off the record". If you don't want to read about it – don't say it.

- If you are ever faced with a crisis, you need to act. There isn't room in this book to discuss all the issues you need to address, so either employ a specialist crisis communications consultant or talk to a reputable PR expert. In a crisis your reputation, brand and image are under threat. It could have cost you £thousands to build them, now is not the time to skimp on protecting them.

Exclusivity

Sometimes if you have an interesting story, journalists will try to get you to agree to "exclusivity". This means that you agree not to give the story to any other media until the date/time agreed with this journalist.

The one rule about exclusivity is: If you agree to it then you MUST stick to it.

If you renege on an exclusivity deal, it will ensure only one thing – complete lack of trust between you and that journalist.

You don't *need* to agree to an exclusivity deal, but if you do, then there must be a benefit in it for you, for example:

- If the journalist won't cover the story unless it is an exclusive.

- If you get a better/larger media "space" (larger spread in paper, longer airtime on radio, etc).

- If you get a guarantee the story will be used, and by what date.

- You get paid!

What if I've already sent a release round to everyone?

If this has happened, you can still agree some "exclusivity" with a particular journalist by giving him/her a little more - e.g. an exclusive interview, providing him with more information, or setting up an exclusive deal on the next story. Of course tell them first that you've already issued the release widely, and then explain the extra exclusive information you will provide for them.

Think of working with journalists as a partnership. Respect them, respect their professionalism and always keep your promises and you won't go far wrong.

The embargo question

An embargo is really not much more than a considered request that a journalist or the media do not publish your press release before the allotted date. The embargo can actually do you a disservice, as it could be that the information is published anyway but without being attributed to you, your company or your client. After all, if the information you have sent out is highly newsworthy, it is the duty of the reporter/media to find out more and to publish!

Normally, if you are going to embargo a release, it is simply a matter of putting the information at the top of the release. Obviously the fact that you have chosen to embargo it means this embargo date is important to you, so ensure it is highly visible, make it bold, highlight it, etc.

For example:

Media release
Issued 20th April 2013, **embargoed until mid-day, 21st April 2013.**

Why embargo?

There are very few good reasons to embargo. As you've seen from the comments from the media, embargoing something can be highly annoying to the media - never a good idea.

Perhaps the only forgivable rationale for an embargo on anything is media/print deadlines. If you need to send out a release on a Thursday, but it can't be made public knowledge until Saturday's media, then an embargo until Saturday is (just about) reasonable. However, with technology and a bit of personal organisation, surely it's possible to issue the release on the Friday to hit Saturday's press!

Advertorials

So, the journalist has said they won't give you any guarantees: "I like the story, but it's down to my editor" is a perfectly legitimate brush-off. After all, the editor has the ultimate decision on what goes in and what stays out.

And even if the journalist or editor says they will definitely use it, there is still no guarantee! All it takes is a story that is more ground-breaking or newsworthy than yours to pip you to the post.

If you absolutely, definitely MUST get your story in the press, then consider the "advertorial."

Think *"cross between editorial and advertisement"* and you have an advertorial.

Advertorials look like editorial but they are paid for, at least in part. (Often you can buy a full page advertorial for much less than you would pay for a full page ad!)

Flick through most glossy magazines and you should find some advertorials.

There is one main rule of advertorial… it must clearly state that it is "advertorial" or "paid-for promotion", or something that makes it absolutely obvious that this is not an impartial editorial opinion.

Advertorials are excellent in that:

- Often they cost less than advertising.

- To the reader they look like editorial, so they also have much of the credibility of editorial.

- You can see and approve the advertorial copy before it is printed (almost never happens with editorial).

- You have a far greater guarantee they will be published, on the date set.

- They are an ideal way of educating people, in a way that would be difficult as a straightforward ad.

Possibly the only downside with an advertorial is that they can sometimes look a little like advertising. To counter this I recommend that you study the "house style" of the publication and aim to imitate it as much as possible. Look at sentence structure, tenses, third person, name styles, etc.

Try to make your advertorial interesting too. Just because you've paid for it doesn't mean you should pump it full of advertising fluff. Make it something that people *want* to read. This is the key to an advertorial piece that really works!

And a really great benefit of an advertorial is that you can often come to an arrangement with the media used, to reprint the advertorial so you can circulate it to your clients and potential clients. Usually advertorials are quite sizeable so it will look like an impressive piece.

Websites and PR

It is important to remember that journalists will visit your website to gather more information about your company.

Bear in mind that the web is an ever-evolving tool. Decide what you expect to gain from your website and be realistic. Also, check out what your clients and journalists expect to see on your website.

While a whiz-bang website with the latest back-office tools is great for a £multi-million dot-com, it is probably totally over the top for a smaller company. But at the very least, your site should be swift to load, informative and interesting. Don't forget to keep it up to date.

Power up your website

Many companies have jumped onto the Website bandwagon without sufficient strategy, only to be disappointed by the results. Online marketing needs a strategy, and websites need to be actively promoted.

You can use your website as part of your PR campaign. Implement the following for greater effectiveness:

- Put your website address on your press releases.

- Make sure your press release is full of powerful SEO key words (ask your web expert which ones are best for your business).

- When you send out a media release, it should also go onto your website (news section) and be put aside to go into your newsletter. Check timing for this - don't mess up any exclusivity deals!

- Any other information of interest to your clients should also go onto the website. But don't expect anyone to look for it, or indeed, to find it for themselves, send out an email to let them know it's there.

- Tell clients about your website in your next newsletter.

- Include information in your company brochure, and put your website address on all your printed material.

- Consider an online pressroom, with downloadable pictures, press release information and even an experts directory with easy-to-find contact information for quotes.

- Put your newsletters online and tell all your clients about them in an email.

- Put a link to your website on your emails. Research has shown this is the most effective way of getting people to visit sites.

- Speak to a website specialist who knows their stuff to get the very latest updates on web technology.

Evaluating PR

Going through these steps may well have raised another question in your mind: "how am I going to measure this?"

Evaluating and measuring PR and its effectiveness is a complicated issue and it can take many years for the full results to come through, from even the smallest PR campaign.

An accepted rule is to measure the media space you achieve, multiply it by three (the worth of editorial compared to advertising) and calculate according to the advertising rates.   But all that will do is help you justify PR to your financial director and the board (of course, that may be all you want to do!) There are other metrics too - for example where you appear on a page or website, which area of the site or media your article is in. What it's next to, etc.

As this book is about practicalities, and as PR should be part of your holistic approach to promoting your business, here is a way to view the effectiveness of your PR and marketing – where it really matters!

Draw up a form like the following, work through how your business is performing at the moment, and how you would like it to perform in the future. In the "vision of the future" column, sit back, put your feet up and start to really dream. Write in your Utopian vision - after all, only you will be reading this!

Add other elements that are of particular interest to you, e.g. employee numbers, unique visits to your website, or how many experts employed.

Sample analysis form for PR evaluation

	As it is now	Future vision
Awareness of Co Name		
Awareness of brand		
Current site engine finds		
Sales figures		
New services/products		
Customer profile		
Geographical spread of clients		

It's true, some elements of the form should involve market research to get a true picture of the facts, but don't be deterred, draw in your perceptions of the answers, then ask other people for their opinions too. This way, although not totally scientific, is highly practical and will probably give you a fairly good idea of each criteria.

Other information, like sales figures and client information, will be readily available

In addition to this holistic approach you will need to keep track of any media coverage you have gained, and then analyse it:

1) By column inches (the traditional method). Compare the amount of space you have received with how much you would normally pay for advertising in that space. (Remember that editorial coverage is generally agreed to be 3 times more valuable than advertising space. And that is conservative!)

2) Assess the circulation of the media, keeping in mind:
- How well does it hit your target audience?
- How positive was the coverage?
- How many of your key messages were mentioned?
- Whether you got any enquiries from it.

3) Keep track of how your clients came to you. Was it through your website, media coverage, advertising, brochures, newsletter or recommendations? Make sure this record is used to assess where the budget will be spent in the next year.

4) Keep track of how many page impressions your website gained. Train up on Analytics to understand your site better.

5) Implement an online satisfaction questionnaire.
- How did visitors find out about the site/company? Is the website useful? If not, why not?   What would they like to see?

6) Track your search engine figures. Do a Google (and other search engines) search on the first day of your campaigns, then hopefully watch it rise each month as more and more online media give you coverage and links.

Although there are numerous ways to evaluate, the most important thing with evaluation is to remember to be totally honest with yourself. Consider what hasn't worked – as well as what has worked. This is vital for making sure you are really making the most of your PR.

You've started so keep going

PR is like a steamroller. It can take a lot of work and energy to get it to start to move, but once it's rolling, it is far easier to keep it going. Once you've got some press coverage it is much easier to keep the media interested in your company.

Keep in contact with the press. Send out regular releases. Think of what else you can do to keep them informed.

Remember: journalists are human. If one has written a great article about your company, pick up the phone and thank them. They really appreciate it when people notice their efforts.

Keep in touch with your friendly journalist - they can be a great source of information! Of course they are busy, but if you can persuade them to come out for lunch, and get to know them, you'll start to reap the rewards!

TIP: If you get a good release printed, or an article featured, copy it and send it out to your target clients. Just in case they didn't see it in the press! (Ensure you obtain the media's permission to copy it first!)

If your release isn't used

If your press release doesn't get picked up and used, don't be disappointed. Most editors receive 1000's of releases every week. They can only use a small percentage. And major national events often take precedence.

So wait until your next event and mail out another release (so long as it is newsworthy). Consistent effort pays off, and consistent appearance in your press will really improve clients' awareness of your company.

Choosing the right PR agency

A major benefit of using a PR company is that they will be totally focused on achieving results for you. Using your company staff usually means they have to fit PR in with the rest of their job – which means that PR often doesn't get the priority it needs.

PR is a pro-active discipline. To do it well needs dedication, imagination, creativity, time, goals, support, knowledge and experience. But the benefits of a great PR campaign can really make the difference to your business. The difference between being seen as a great company – or not being seen at all!

If you feel that you would prefer to find out about the advantages of employing a PR consultancy, then here are a few things you should consider:

- When choosing an agency, think about the companies you admire for their PR activity, and ask them who they use. Call up your trade or local media too - which agencies would they recommend?

- Think about a fixed-fee. Many agencies will provide their services within a fixed cost.

- Be prepared to go for a campaign, rather than just a one-hit-wonder. There is no point in getting loads of coverage for one story, then disappearing again into obscurity. However, there is much to be said for trying out an agency on a project – with the proviso that if it is successful, you will extend the arrangement.

- Acknowledge you are going to have to get involved. Appointing an agency is a combination of partner working and delegation. It is not abdication!   Be prepared to spend time with the agency, get them up to speed with your company, and keep on feeding them information.

- Consider forming a "contract of expectations". This will solve so many problems that arise from people making incorrect assumptions.   Things that would go into your contract of expectations could include:

   ~ Agreed number of press releases to be written and sent each month.
    ~ That the agency will give you prompt feedback on results (what does prompt mean to you?)
    ~ That the agency is pro-active and comes up with ideas for you.

- Find out who your main contact will be at the agency. Is it the same person who pitched for the account? (So often the directors will pitch, and you end up with the office junior).

- Don't be fooled by agency staff that say they know all the right journalists. That may well be the case, but if they aren't creative, or capable of writing a good release, they may never get you in the press, no matter how many editors they know.

- Have a good look through their portfolio. Find out what they have done for other clients. Ask them about the rationale behind the project, and the negatives of the campaign as well as the positives.

- After they have proved they are experienced with other clients, you want to know what they will do for you. So ask them to present a few ideas.

- Make a judgement call on the type of PR company you need. Do you need a specialist, like finance PR, or a governmental lobbyist? Or do you need someone with great expertise in crisis management?

- Listen to the agency. If they make a suggestion, or have a viewpoint on something, then take it into account.   With all due respect, the chances are they have tried out similar campaigns before and they know the likely pitfalls and outcomes.

- Finally, make absolutely certain you get on well with your account manager. It is vital that you are both on the same wavelength and can communicate well.

- With the internet, email, Skype and numerous communications tools, it's possible to deal with a PR company many miles away. However beware of going too far afield; a fundamental requirement of PR is a deep understanding of the region's culture, the industry and the media - which is why international companies will often appoint a PR agency for every country or region where they work.

No Superheroes required!

Let's finish this book by dispelling one final myth: writing a great press release does NOT require superpowers! You don't have to start changing in phone-booths nor wear your underpants on the outside of your clothes!

Whether you're a business owner who wants to appoint an agency, a sole-trader who's decided to try PR for themselves, or if you are an employee appointed to handle your company's PR, then congratulations!   Public Relations is one of the most exciting, fast-paced, creative and rewarding marketing tools around. I urge you make the most of it.

Writing releases is just one part of your role in PR, and fortunately it's a part that is simply a process; following the steps in this book should mean you are fully tooled up and ready to write killer press releases.

Your mission, should you choose to accept, is simply to make a start and write your first press release this week. Whether it results in show-stopping media coverage, or simply a great first draft, congratulations on taking the first step to join the many thousands of PR Superstars already enjoying the power of PR!

PR Jargon Buster

Press Release
A one or two page (certainly no more than three) informative piece of writing that is produced to be sent to the press or media. It is never sent out unless the client or business owner/director has fully approved it in advance.

A press release is written loosely in the style of the publications it will be sent to. The aim of the Press Release is to create interest, and offer the media something they can print as it is, or to edit to fit their title. However, there is NO GUARANTEE that this will happen; many releases simply find their way into a deep dark bin surrounded by hundreds of other releases received that day. This is why I would advise *gently* pre-calling the key titles by phone.

Photocall
An invitation to the media to attend a particularly interesting or high-visibility event that is either "news" or that will make a great photo. There are rules and issues concerning photocalls, like making sure that you deal with the possibility of competing newspapers coming along at the same time.

Editorial

All text that is printed in the media, except advertising, comes under the term "Editorial". Whether it is a news article or a feature, editor's comments or letters page.

News Article or Item

News is something that is "new". Or something that passes the "-est" test: biggest, best, oldest, largest, etc.

The news media will print or broadcast "news". The news may have come from a press release, or from their own sources (e.g. courts, tip-offs, observations, etc). News can take the form of articles or short "News in Brief" snippets. News can also be in the form of a captioned photograph (see photocall above). A news article will be written by a journalist or an editor (though it could be an un-edited copy of the press release).

Feature Stories

A feature is a longer article, which examines a product, company or a personality in depth. It is often a 'warts and all' profile, which may also make comparisons about a company or product with others in the same sector.

Although it covers more space in the publication there is no guarantee it will attract more readers. Many people under pressure will skim papers and magazines to glean the main points of an article. However it does contribute to increasing a company's profile and also wins respect from others in the industry for allowing such open access.

Case Study
This is also a longer article, which takes an in-depth look at a particular project and details the challenges presented during its implementation. It is another 'warts and all' profile and is usually placed in very specialist publications.

Column.
A standard measurement of newsprint text. (Most newspapers have 7, 8 or 11 columns across the width of their page.)
In editorial terms, a "column" can also be an ongoing agreement between the media and a writer, where the writer will provide information on topical events, etc, with a slant from their own expertise.

Columns by famous or high profile writers, are sometimes commissioned and paid for by the media, or they can be written free of charge by the writer. It all depends on the benefit to the writer and the benefit to the media.

Advertorial

A cross between an advert and editorial. Quite often this is a good way to get editorial into a newspaper, particularly if your editorial is not very news-worthy.

Usually one pays for the advertising element and negotiates an adjoining editorial space free of charge.

Competitions.

Reader competitions can be negotiated with the media. Often there is no charge to the client, except that they provide the prize. With many competitions, the client gets the chance to see copy before it goes to print, and also to negotiate the exact size/space they will get.

Readers Offers.

Where readers of a certain media get a special deal. E.g. 20% off a cruise, etc. These are negotiated with the media. Normally they will entail a voucher/coupon that is to be redeemed.

JOURNALISTS:

Trade journalists are usually quite specialised in their field and probably know as much about your industry as you do. You won't fool them or their readers with exaggerated information, but you will receive coverage for items that wouldn't make the wider press services.

National reporters will usually have a quick grasp of your field if they don't already know a little. They are very questioning and up against tight deadlines, especially for the dailies. They work very quickly and will have a simplistic yet accurate approach, which is targeted at a diverse readership. They need to be approached with material in plain English.

Local reporters are often more interested in what's happening on their doorstep – a company that's creating jobs, launching a new product, investing in the local community. Local reporters will probably have a great knowledge of your area, and be a wonderful source of information. Often newspapers will be weeklies, which means deadlines are not quite as tight as dailies, however this is counteracted by the fact that many local newspapers only employ a few reporters to cover a wide area.

THE MEDIA

Broadsheets
Larger newspapers, e.g. The Times. Frequently nationals, but some regionals are broadsheet format.

Tabloids
Refers initially to the size of smaller newspapers, e.g. The Mirror. Until the Independent launched in tabloid size, the term was also used to define a certain sector of newspaper.

Nationals
Any newspaper covering the "nation" - and frequently beyond, e.g. The Telegraph, etc.

Regionals
Any newspaper that covers a geographical region or area, e.g. The Manchester Evening News or The Birmingham Post.

Trade Press
Magazines or newspapers that are specific to a certain trade. E.g. Pig Breeders Monthly. Often available on subscription or free. Hardly ever found in newsagents.

Weeklies, Dailies, Monthlies
Issued on this basis, as the name suggests.

Broadcast Media

Includes TV, Radio and Internet media (e.g. portals, magazine sites, blogs, etc)

Blogs

Often run by very enthusiastic experts who really know their stuff. Great influencing power so make sure you analyse the blogs in your sector and send them PR too!

Online media

With lesser costs to publish than the print media, you can often score here with press releases that fail to meet the traditional press. Online media can include blogs, or internet sites for print magazines, or even standalone internet magazines/media. The formats can vary tremendously, and they can include radio, video or copywritten text.

Frequently a fast-moving media, and most likely to be interested in content, good photographs and even video.

About the Author

With a background in sales, marketing and PR, working within client companies and agencies, including Shandwick (the World's largest PR group) Susan Haswell established her own PR consultancy in February 1997.

She has worked on an impressive client list, including Cosmopolitan™ Licensed Products, Georgia Pacific, Clarity Technology for Sun Microsystems and National Express. She has also worked with smaller businesses, not-for-profit organisations, Government organisations and community initiatives, and handled many product and brand launches.

Having worked for clients of all sizes, and launching several businesses of her own, Susan firmly believes that PR is for everyone, regardless of their budget.

"PR is a seriously powerful business tool. It is often assumed PR is the province of the larger organisation, but often it can be a catalyst for success for the start-up business, voluntary organisations or companies with limited budget."

Susan now lives and works in Devon. In addition to writing books, working with clients and running training courses, Susan also works on several voluntary campaigns on ecological and environmental issues.

For more information: www.bigresults.co.uk
sue.h@bigresults.co.uk